DESTINY CALLED TO THEM

By Beverley Baxter

OXFORD UNIVERSITY PRESS

London   New York   Toronto

ILLUSTRATIONS

DESTINY
CALLED
TO THEM

Chapter One

A MOTOR-CAR SWIRLED UP TO THE ENTRANCE OF 145 Piccadilly as the police cleared a free passage for it. In the grey of a London December morning a small crowd of spectators stopped to look.

The door of the car was opened by the chauffeur and a young man got out. His face was deathly serious. The spectators, recognizing the Duke of York, raised their hats and one or two even applauded; for when a national crisis is on the true Londoner regards the principal participants rather as actors who deserve encouragement.

For once the Duke made no attempt to recognize the good-humored tribute of the crowd. He did not see it. His eyes were looking into a world of their own, a world of endless crowds and cruel loneliness, a world of pomp in which the slave would play the Emperor, a world from which there could be no release save for a few hours at a time.

Almost like a sleep-walker he made his way to the door of 145 and disappeared into it. The crowd moved on and walked a little faster to restore its congealed circulation.

An intimate friend has described what took place inside. The house at 145 Piccadilly was more than just a home. Though supremely a home it was also the headquarters of a very busy servant of the State. There was Sir Basil Brook, Comptroller of the Household. There were secretaries; and on normal days visitors, officials and friends came in an endless stream. Somewhere in the midst of the incessant activity of the house the Duke and Duchess and their children contrived to live a happy family life.

But for the last three or four days the house had been growing increasingly quiet. Everybody was waiting for the final decision on the abdication. The machinery of official life had slowed down until the wheels were barely turning. Instead of the incessant traffic of secretaries, visitors and friends, the house had grown silent, almost as if someone had died. When the Duke entered his house that morning he made straight for the morning-room on the left of the ground-floor just beyond the Comptroller's office. The Duchess of York was waiting for him and her eyes were wide with sympathy and understanding.

The little Princesses came from the garden where they had been playing. Sometimes they went to Buckingham Palace to ride, but during the last few days they had remained in their own place in Piccadilly. Something was happening that they did not understand and it was interfering with their lives. With the exuberance of children and the feeling that everything would turn out all right they rushed to the morning-room to greet their parents. A few moments later they came out and went wonderingly to their nursery. Something had happened. They did not know what it was, and stranger than anything else their mother did not seem to want them to be there while she and her husband were talking.

Why was their mother so serious? Why had their father looked at them and said nothing? The endless, sunless day drew to its close. The lamps of Piccadilly were lit and the darkness of evening replaced the grey gloom of what had once been a day.

The time came for the Princesses to go to bed. They went up to the morning-room to say good-night. With the dogged optimism of the young, which believes everything will right itself somehow, they felt they could almost certainly persuade their mother to tell them the story of the wicked pony at St. Paul's Waldenbury—or perhaps their father would make up a little play for them to act.

They did not realize that a play had been written in which all four of them would act until the final curtain of their lives. There was no good-night joke, no bed-time story. Puzzled and bewildered, the children went to bed with such thoughts as children have when life is beyond their comprehension.

In the morning-room the Duchess turned to her

Prince Albert aboard a warship in 1914.
—Spencer Arnold

husband, who was standing silently by the window.

'When will David's abdication be announced?' she asked in a voice that was hardly more than a whisper.

'On Thursday, in the House of Commons,' he replied.

Thus, strangely and unexpectedly, Destiny called this man and his wife to the throne.

'The King is dead. Long live the King!'

There was no such cry when George VI took over the monarchy vacated by Edward VIII, the king who was never crowned. Never in the long history of England had a sovereign ascended the throne in conditions so difficult and bewildering as on that Saturday in December when the succession of George VI was proclaimed.

I went to see the official proclamation from the battlements of St. James's Palace. It was raining in a desultory way when the trumpets rang out and the heralds in their gorgeous uniforms read the proclamation.

There was no thrill about it. Less than a year before I had stood in the same courtyard when the death of King George V and the succession of his eldest son, the Prince of Wales, was announced.

There was magnificence and tradition about that, a mingling of sorrow and rejoicing, tribute to what is gone and cheers for what lies ahead.

A king had died, and a nation mourned, but the monarchy went on, thus typifying the indestructible continuity of the life of the nation itself.

Contrast that with the atmosphere less than a year later when the trumpeters and heralds had to proclaim, not the death of a king, but the renunciation of a throne; and the succession, not of the eldest son by the unalterable decree of birth, but of the younger brother after discussion, compromise and conference.

The Duke of York, as far as we can say of one in his position, was little known at the period when the ab-

dication crisis broke over Britain. He had been content to be the younger son of the King, fulfilling such duties as were required of him both at home and in the outer Empire, but never seeking or, for that matter, attracting the limelight.

He was devoted to his elder brother but neither envied nor coveted his instinctive gift of the spectacular. Incidentally Edward had the greatest respect for the character of the Duke of York, which he generously recognized as stronger than his own. To this day, even with so many difficult influences at work, the affection and mutual respect of the two brothers remains unchanged.

As young men there was a touch of rivalry between them which few suspected. Edward was determined to be a first-class golfer and worked hard at the game. When he became an eleven handicap the newspapers heralded it as an event of national importance. He won a competition and sent a telegram of congratulation to his teacher.

But there was one thing which dimmed the mirror of his glory. His brother Albert, who never bothered much about golf, had a handicap of nine and with very little trouble could have come down to scratch. The newspapers knew nothing of this family rivalry. Albert never played in tournaments. He just shot a consistent 81-83 and was content.

Edward went at his sports with great dash and alternate enthusiasm or despair. They played tennis together but Edward discarded the game after a time in favor of hunting and golf. Albert became almost a first-class tennis player. In fact he advanced so far that he entered the men's doubles at Wimbledon. He and his partner Commander Louis (now Sir Louis) Greig made a good fight of it before they were knocked out.

Edward always seemed the younger of the two, with his eagerness and his boyish desire to excel. Wherever he turned he found his brother Albert the senior in

Queen Elizabeth when she was still Lady Elizabeth Bowes-Lyon, 1906. From a miniature.

—Spencer Arnold.

practical experience and efficiency. In fairness one must admit that the strain imposed by their public duties was far more severe on the Prince of Wales than on the Duke of York. It would have been easily understandable if he had been a fumbler at games with very little interest in his prowess or lack of it. Instead of that, however, there was a tempestuous desire to succeed if only 'to put Bertie in his place.'

The ordinary 'scenes' of family life between the boys and their father were not infrequent. King George V had no doubt at all as to who was the head of the Royal household. As for parental authority it was a subject which brooked no discussion.

One holiday-time when they were all at Sandringham King George was checking up on church attendance and found that his three older sons were missing. Sending for Sir Louis Greig he banged the table with his fist and roared:

'I'll take no excuses. As long as I am the King and their father these young rascals have damned well got to go to church every Sunday morning!'

It is no secret that the Prince of Wales and the Duke of Kent chafed under this parental authority. The other two brothers accepted it. Perhaps it was because the Duke of York had spent so many years in the Navy and the Duke of Gloucester so many in the Army that, at any rate as men, they realized that respect for authority is part of the price that must be paid for enjoyment of human liberty.

Yet the present King, as a youth, did not accept the laws of the Medes and Persians without an outbreak now and then.

Once when he was an undergraduate at Cambridge he was found smoking a pipe while wearing a cap and gown. An officious mentor pointed out how his offence was aggravated by his being a member of the Royal family.

'We're not a family,' said the young Prince bitterly, 'we're a firm.'

In those words there was the instinctive protest of a young man who had little love for the pomp and circumstance of Royalty. Power he respected and authority he recognized; but he could not rise to Shakespeare's argument, 'There is a Divinity that doth hedge a King.'

Yet how true those words were he was to learn many years later. Unsought, unplanned, he was to see a hedge placed about him that would rob him for ever from normal contact with his fellows.

*King George VI, as Midshipman when he was still
Prince Albert, with Admiral Sir Lewis Beaumont and
the Commander of the Royal Yacht, 1912.*
                                    —Spencer Arnold.

Chapter Two

PRINCE ALBERT FACED LIFE WITH A SERIOUS AFFLIC-tion. He stammered, and so ordinary conversation was a trial to him and accentuated his shyness. His affliction was like Arnold Bennett's. For no particular reason a certain consonant would hold up the nerve-centers, and a long and agonizing silence would occur in the midst of perfect normal speech.

Perhaps it was this shyness which created a special sympathy between the boy and his father. There was no doubt in anyone's mind as to which was the favorite son of George V.

It was no wonder then that George V, the 'Sailor King,' should want his favorite son to go into the Navy. Therefore, at the age of fourteen, the boy was sent as a naval cadet to Osborne, with strict instructions that he should be treated exactly the same as everyone else and that any preferential treatment would be viewed as disregarding the King's wishes.

Shortly after his arrival at Osborne there was an oral examination of an elementary nature. Gazing at Albert, the examiner asked abruptly: 'What is the afterpart of a ship called?'

The young Prince rose to his feet. He knew the answer, of course. But alas, when he tried to say 'the quarter-deck,' the consonant q held him up. He blushed with embarrassment and was morose for some time afterwards.

As time went on he determined that he would conquer the defect. He studied how to avoid pitfalls and spoke of 'my father' or 'His Majesty,' but never 'the King.' He was giving the consonant k a wide berth. 'I shall get the better of this,' he said over and over again, and practised speaking hour in and hour out until he declared that he could not stand the sound of his own voice. His conversation grew more easy all the time, but any formal occasion set him back and he felt the cruel pangs of discouragement.

But only for a moment. 'Invictus' was in his blood and he fought on.

For four years Prince Albert studied at Osborne and later at Dartmouth. Discipline was severe and the work was hard, for already our fighting ships were becoming huge floating mechanisms. Engineering took up more and more of the curriculum. From class-room to engine-room and from engine-room to class-room the future King of England pursued his studies. To-day, when he goes into a great industrial factory, he does not smile and say 'What does this thing do?' as he points at some part of a gigantic machine. He is thrilled by machinery and is profoundly interested and well informed in the development of industrial science. What is more, it has given him an understanding of the minds of the men who work at the machines.

And then the first big excitement of his life! At eighteen years of age he was attached to H.M.S. *Cumberland* for its customary cruise. Life was full of interest. There was the companionship of his mess-mates in the gun-room, lots of work and lots of fun, dancing in strange ports, playing polo in the West Indies, putting in at Newfoundland and sailing up the St. Lawrence to Quebec.

Alas! At Ottawa he contracted measles, which annoyed him considerably. It was too bad because Canada had been a country which had always fascinated the children of the Royal Family.

On duty on the ship and in the gun-room he was 'Mr. Johnston.' Here is a routine report on him by one of his seniors: 'Cheerful and thorough. Handles the picket-boat particularly well when in charge.'

And then the war! As a sub-lieutenant he went into action in the fore-turret of the *Collingwood* in the epic Battle of Jutland.

Today the tactics of that battle still divide theorists and sever friendships. Was Jellicoe right to play safe or would Beatty, if he had been in Jellicoe's place, have sent every German ship to the bottom?

These higher questions of strategy did not worry Sub-lieutenant Johnston unduly. He had his job to

*The Duke of York as an officer in the Royal Air Force
shortly after the World War.*

—Photo by Downey.

do and the *Collingwood* was being hotly engaged.

It was the *Collingwood* that helped to cripple the *Derfflinger* when that German cruiser fought its heroic battle to help cover Von Scheer's famous wheeling maneuver.

Buckingham Palace is full of priceless gifts received over the centuries. The wealth of India and the Orient and the artistry of Europe have all combined to fill the rooms of the Palace with jewelled swords and golden statuary. But the possession which King George cherishes above all others is a fading white ensign which flew at the *Collingwood's* masthead at the Battle of Jutland.

There was, however, a harder battle which Sub-lieutenant Johnston had to fight. Gastric trouble, as a result of illness contracted on his early voyages, had developed. Four times he was invalided out of the Navy and four times he returned to duty. At last the realization came to him that his health would no longer permit him to pursue a naval career. He was heart-broken. His ambitions had soared high. He saw himself rising to high place in the Senior Service and spending his manhood in the company of the men and ships that he loved.

Every man has his secret battle to fight. Albert George had two—his speech and his health. 'But I shall not be beaten,' he said again and again. He was operated on for appendicitis and on recovery at once joined the Royal Naval air-station at Cranwell. Later he went to the Royal Air Force and took his pilot's certificate, being given the rank of Captain and then Wing Commander.

So the war came to an end. Dressed in the uniform of the Royal Air Force, Albert George crossed to the Continent and rode beside the King of the Belgians on his triumphal return to Brussels.

Great moments . . . sad moments. . . . A world had died and a new and more strident world had been born . . . a new world of hysteria and crude freedom. . . . A world of jazz and speed and changing values, a world determined to drown the memories of the war by living stridently and dancing to jungle music.

'The lamps of Europe are going out,' cried Sir Edward Grey in August 1914. 'We shall not see them lit again in our time.'

But the younger son of the King looked ahead with courage and saw life and work ahead of him. He was older than his years and serious.

Like so many of his generation he had lived a lifetime in the crash and fury of world war.

On December 14th, 1918, he celebrated his twenty-third birthday. The boy had become a man. Some day he would be married to a foreign princess—a prospect that made him shrug his shoulders. Slowly he faced the fact that the Navy and Air Force had made him free. Now the claims of his position were fastening on him like chains.

Still he was only twenty-three and at that age it is sufficient just to be alive. One thing is certain. He had no thoughts then for a little Scottish girl named Lady Elizabeth Bowes-Lyon. She was a friend of his sister and he had met her. But when he had gone to the war in 1914 she was only fourteen.

And men of nineteen don't notice little girls as young as that.

The Duke of York at the Belvoir
Hunt Meet at Croxton Park in
1921.

—Spencer Arnold.

The Duke of York on his favor-
te polo pony.

—Vandyk.

Chapter Three

ELIZABETH BOWES-LYON WAS THE YOUNGEST DAUGH-ter of a family of ten. That is important. To achieve individuality in a family of brothers and sisters as large as that one must be a peace-maker, a diplomat or a bully. Lady Elizabeth had neither the nature nor the size to be a bully.

She was definitely for peace and diplomacy. In fact, as so often happens in a soviet of brothers and sisters, there is one who is accepted as unbiassed and fair and who is therefore invested with considerable authority. Such a one was the little Scottish girl who was to be the future Queen of England.

She was a favorite with the whole family as well as with her parents. With that kind sentimentality which characterizes the Scot, she was called 'the Smiling Lassie' by the retainers of Glamis Castle, the ancient and haunted Highland home of the Bowes-Lyons.

There was no nonsense about the young lady's mother. The Countess of Strathmore had all the Scot's admiration for the eternal things of life. Therefore she wanted her children to be good, to be honest, to be kind, to be intelligent—and to obey their parents at all times.

Another thing that the Countess believed was that a woman should be womanly. By that she meant not only that a young lady should be trained to be a good wife and mother but that she should be trained in those arts which add charm and luster.

Thus did the youthful Elizabeth learn to sit at an easel and paint. No-one will pretend that her talent was outstanding, but she had a natural feeling for color and her studies made her increasingly sensitive to form, design, and shades of color.

She also studied the piano and not only played quite charmingly but acquired a deep and genuine interest in the rich literature of classical music.

Then there was French to learn, for many foreigners came to Glamis and the daughters of the house must have at least one other language in which to converse with their guests who must be made to feel at home.

That this is an important asset for a person in public life is obvious. Everyone remembers how charmed the French people were last summer, when the King and Queen visited Paris, with the Queen's ability to talk beautifully and fluently in their own tongue. Barriers immediately fall, and understanding can develop rapidly, when conversation flows easily.

Nor did the education end there.

There was the world of books—and the Countess expected that her children would have a knowledge of and a liking, if possible, for the classics of literature.

Finally Elizabeth had to be completely at home on a horse in the hunting-field and prepared to spend hours in the open air in all weathers.

The family life which the Strathmores and their family lived alternated between Scotland and their country house down south in Herefordshire.

In this study of the characters of the King and Queen of England I am painting a portrait from real life, not from the imagination of a courtier. I want to show them as they are, two young people of flesh and blood like the rest of us, facing the future as everyone must do, knowing that winter-time and summer-time, blossom-time and harvest-time, come to king and peasant alike, realizing that joy and disappointment and the severance of companionships enter unbidden into the palace as well as the cottage.

No-one could foresee the future of Elizabeth of Glamis Castle. Although she was descended from that mighty figure King Robert the Bruce, the wildest imagination could not have pictured her on the throne of Great Britain. Yet if the Earl and Countess of Strathmore could have foreseen that future they could not have trained her better for the task. Gentle, cultured, beautifully spoken, unselfish, serious and joyous—was this not a girl fit to be a queen?

When her fourteenth birthday approached she became highly excited. Her father had promised her a

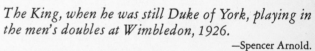

*The King, when he was still Duke of York, playing in
the men's doubles at Wimbledon, 1926.*

—Spencer Arnold.

*The King driving in the Generals versus the Admirals
Golf Match in 1934.*

—Spencer Arnold.

theater party in London, with a whole box to themselves!

The discussions as to the choice of the play were endless. There had to be a new frock of course, and a supper in town before going to the play. This was to be a birthday she would never forget.

The great night came. In an almost empty theater the actors went through their parts with the voices and actions of automatons. The streets outside were seething with wildly excited mobs making their way towards Buckingham Palace.

Little Elizabeth Bowes-Lyon sat in the box and tried to smile. Her older brother was there and he was staring into space as if looking into another world.

It was the evening of August 4th, 1914. Britain's ultimatum to Germany would expire at midnight.

In the four years that lay ahead the nature of the future Queen was to be softened and enriched by contact with the heroism and sacrifice of war. Glamis Castle was turned into a hospital for overseas' soldiers, principally Australian. The youngest daughter of the house played her part like a ministering angel, not only relieving the monotony of long hours of pain but, in turn, listening over and over again to the thrilling story of how these men had had such a vision of the British Empire that they had come across the seas of their own free will to offer their lives in its defence.

When off duty she drove in a dog-cart to the houses of the villagers and cottagers whose sons were fighting in the fierce, proud regiments of Scotland. She sat with the bereaved wife and mother and she gave hope to those who dreaded the coming of each day.

She still smiled but there was wistfulness in her smile now, a tenderness that was born of human understanding. One day she was saying good-bye to an Australian who was being evacuated for duty once more.

He was tongue-tied and awkward, but with a grin he pointed to a placard tied to his great-coat. It read:

'En route to Berlin. If injured in transit please return to Glamis Castle.'

Of such incidents was the fabric of her girlhood spun. But experience went deeper than that. There was the day when news came that her adored brother had been killed serving with his regiment. And there came another day when her second brother, a mere boy in uniform, was posted as 'missing.' Two others were serving in the line, for none had held back.

Glamis Castle, that place of endless legend, looked down and gathered more memories to its heart.

August 4th, 1915.

August 4th, 1916.

August 4th, 1917.

August 4th, 1918.

Four more birthdays and the child of fourteen was a woman of eighteen. Armistice Night came and the people stampeded into the streets.

The stampede went on for months. As if to forget the war, London became dance mad. Women found their freedom and, like the slaves of the South after the victory of the Federal forces, they didn't know what to do with it.

The streets were full of broken men feeling their weary way along the cruel cobbled roads of peace, but the night-clubs were packed with men and women whose feet moved faster and faster to the rhythm of trumpets, saxophones and drums.

It was the age of speed, the age of forgetfulness, the age of swift profits, a cruel shoddy age of sham sparkle and imitation wit, an age where love lasted for an hour and the cocktail was a symbol.

'We live in new times,' said the younger generation as they relegated the wisdom of their parents to the limbo of far-off forgotten things.

Lady Elizabeth Bowes-Lyon went little to London. 'I prefer the country,' she said, and was content.

The Duke of York deep sea fishing in the Bay of Islands, New Zealand, 1927.

—Spencer Arnold.

Chapter Four

IN 1920 THERE WAS A HOUSE-PARTY AT GLAMIS. THE Countess of Strathmore was ill and it fell to the lot of Lady Elizabeth to act as hostess.

The guests included her friend Princess Mary and her brother Albert, who had just been created 'Duke of York, Earl of Inverness and Baron Killarney.' No longer was 'Mr. Johnston' a prince. He had joined the tiny circle of Royal Dukes, which did not alter him in the slightest.

It was this house-party that began the business. The young Duke was charmed with his hostess. And Elizabeth? Well, it was pleasant to find that her friend Mary should have so nice a brother.

Of course it was Princess Mary's wedding in 1922 that finally completed the mischief—the old romantic combination of the bride's favorite brother and the favorite bridesmaid that once more insured the one wedding being a forerunner of another. Lady Elizabeth was much admired at the wedding and for the first time the newspapers became conscious of her existence.

But no-one admired her or noticed her as much as the Duke of York. The young man was deeply and irretrievably in love.

One Sunday in January 1923 the Duke was staying at the Strathmore's lovely English country house, 'St. Paul's Waldenbury.' It was here that Elizabeth had been born and had spent much of her girlhood before the exigencies of war made Glamis her permanent home.

Even the month of January could not obliterate the charm of the pleasant Queen Anne house, which in summer is almost covered in honeysuckle and magnolia. At the end of the garden there is an enchanted wood, there are fields to wander in, and there is a roaring fire for wet days when the very ill temper of the weather adds to the good humor inside the house.

But better than all these things, better than the books and the good companionship and the view from the windows, was the presence of the youngest daughter of the house—or so thought the Duke of York.

Now on this particular Sunday morning I regret to record that the Duke and Lady Elizabeth did not go to church. They went for a country walk instead. Perhaps they visited the enchanted wood. More likely they had no particular idea where they went. At any rate when they returned for luncheon their faces deceived no-one.

They were overwhelmed with congratulations while the future King and Queen stood side by side feeling rather foolish, terribly happy and thrilled.

The engagement was not entirely a surprise to King George and Queen Mary, but it was a historic break with precedent. Not since the year 1100 had Scotland supplied a queen to the English throne and it was hundreds of years since a prince of England in direct line of succession to the throne had been allowed to marry one of His Majesty's subjects.

The whole thing was thoroughly symptomatic of the character of the Duke of York. He was never a rebel, he never quarrelled with the established order of things, but within his acceptance of those limitations to his freedom he demanded the right to live as a man. To that extent he shared a common purpose with his brother the Prince of Wales.

Both married for love. Both broke with precedent. Yet it cost the one his throne while the other was to see his wife crowned as Queen of England. It was Fate.

However, the Duke of York neither feared nor found opposition at home. Both King George and Queen Mary placed character and womanliness above all else in the choice of wives for their sons. And how better could the Duke have chosen than by taking the young woman of Glamis Castle, of whom a great friend had written:

'She possesses an unselfish nature, simple and affectionate; a mind and character incapable of unkindness of thought or unkindness of action; a complete lack of affectation or pose; a sincerity and gentleness.'

It would be wrong to say that the marriage of the

The King and Queen aboard the Royal Yacht Britannia *at the Royal Thames Yacht Club Races, 1935.*
—Spencer Arnold.

Duke and Duchess of York, three months later, threw the nation into a frenzy of excitement. The Duke's visits abroad and his years in the Navy had not made him an intimate figure to the public. Besides, in the realm of popular adulation, the Prince of Wales left no room for any of his brothers. That is not meant unkindly—on the contrary. For Edward would have been glad to have escaped some of this publicity. But the camera, the news-reel and the microphone had caught him and would not let him go. He was regarded by the women of the world as a sort of Royal film star. When he was in the picture there were eyes for no-one else.

And if it be true that the Duke of York was to some extent an unknown quantity, his bride was almost totally unknown. She had never been photographed standing on skis at St. Moritz; she had never been photographed playing the tables at Monte Carlo, or listening to a torch-singer at the Café de Paris. She had never been part of the younger set which only came to life at the cocktail hour and danced until dawn with young men with no chins.

Nor was she a foreign Princess with an exotic name like Anastasia and endless archdukes as relations. It is not as romantic for a bride to travel by train from Scotland as it is for her to come on a battle-cruiser while the maternal heart of the British nation opens to embrace the daughter from over the sea.

Nevertheless the wedding was a tremendous affair. There was one at least among the thousands who was full of excitement. I refer to the author of this book, who was sent to the Abbey to write a description of the ceremony for his newspaper.

All the great ones of the realm were there. Mr. Asquith and his wife actually smiled at Mr. Lloyd George, which shows what a softening effect romance has on human nature. Lloyd George was as full of vivacity as if it were his wedding instead of the Duke's. Bonar Law moved to his seat with a quiet, sad dignity that nothing could dispel. Only a few months later his body would be brought to the same place, while the music of grief would take the place of Mendelssohn's *Wedding March*.

The guests came in an endless procession—moustached generals ablaze with medals, hook-nosed, six-foot women with vintage ermine on their shoulders, young guardsmen with unobtrusive but perfect moustaches, judges, Ministers of State, and every now and then a face of such beauty that it set the pulses tingling. There were Indian princes, ambassadors, Crown princes, and here and there a tall, soldierly, sunburned figure to remind us that there is always a job of work being done in a far-flung empire.

In the Chancel the two families are divided. On one side there are the King and Queen keenly and democratically interested in the whole affair, there is the Princess Royal with her husband, the Royal brothers, the Duke of Connaught and all the rest of the cousins, uncles and aunts which make one family much the same as any other.

On the other side there are the chieftains of the bride's clan and their women. The men are dressed in traditional ceremonial Highland costume and their jet-black heads are raised imperiously as if to say: 'Aye, the bridegroom is the son of the King, but the bride has the blood of the ancient kings of Scotland in her veins.'

So with the sun streaming through Cathedral windows and with the music of the choir reaching the very rafters, the tall, slim Prince of England was married to the gentle, smiling daughter of Scotland. They drove away to the friendly cheers of the London crowd. The politicians went back to their place across the Square and the generals went home to loosen their belts in preparation for a belated lunch.

Two threads of destiny had been woven and were joined in one. It was a fateful moment in the life of the nation when these two young people, who so well and truly loved each other, received the benediction of the sun that shone on England's pageantry that April morning.

The Royal Yacht Britannia.

—Spencer Arnold.

Chapter Five

AFTER THEIR MARRIAGE THE WORLD HEARD LITTLE OF the Duke and Duchess of York for the excellent reason that they did not seek the limelight. I remember seeing them one night shortly after their marriage at the Embassy Club, which was in those days a meeting-place for London's smart set. They were guests of Lady Cunard, the American-born London hostess, and the Prince of Wales was in the party as well.

The Prince danced with his sister-in-law and all the most elegant necks of Mayfair stretched themselves to look at the little Duchess.

The Queen's beauty of face is difficult to capture by camera. The term 'photogenic,' so dear to cinema pro-ducers, could hardly be applied to her, yet everyone who has seen her in real life exclaims over her loveli-ness and deplores the inaccurate impression her photo-graphs convey of her charm. Like the princess in the fairy-tale, she has hair as black as ebony, eyes as blue as the sky, and a peaches-and-cream complexion. The French, however, would probably call her beauty *spirituel,* since it springs from the quick change of feeling in a mobile face, rather than from classic fea-tures. It has its source in animation, vivacity and sym-pathy, themselves the natural expression of an alert, intelligent and sensitive mind.

I don't think that the Duke and Duchess ever went to the Mecca of Mayfair again. Their estimate of it was probably the same as that of the famous dramatist, J. B. Priestley, who in his most recent play depicts Hades—and places it in a night-club.

The truth is that the Duke was serious of purpose and that the Duchess was a real person. They could not have played the smart set game if they had wanted to, and most decidedly they did not want to.

On the other hand they were enormously excited by a sociological experiment which the Duke had made as a bachelor and which was growing in strength.

Ever since his college days at Cambridge, where he had made a special study of history and economics, he had had a sincere and vital interest in economic theory and sociology, based on extensive reading and investi-gation.

He believed that it would be a very good thing for the sons of the rich to mingle with the sons of the poor. Equally so, he wanted the sons of the poor to mix with the sons of the rich if only to remind them-selves that they were all descended from Adam.

Not an easy project to carry out, but the Duke hit on a plan.

He would take 200 boys from the exclusive private schools of Britain, which are paradoxically known as 'public schools,' and 200 boys from the elementary schools where the sons of workmen are educated. They would spend a week together at the Duke of York's seaside camp, where no distinction would be made of any kind.

It was a noisy and overwhelming success from the start. The Duke attended each year (and still does) and joined in the games and the sing-songs. Class dis-tinction was kept outside the camp boundaries. The camp is one of the most significant things in British life. That a blow at the rigid caste system should have come from a prince of the blood is something which the future historian may have to note.

Further than that, the Duke became the President of the Industrial Welfare Society and absorbed him-self in the life of the working people. Perhaps it was not entirely unselfishness, because his love of machin-ery had been kindled in the Navy and, to him, a factory was a fascinating thing to study at first-hand.

All this in the 1920's, quietly and unostentatiously, with no limelight or publicity to glorify their efforts.

For every formal visit to the industrial centers he, and often the Duchess, made many informal ones. Then they would stroll casually about the workers' houses, the future Queen chatting with the girls and mothers and the future King hearing first hand from the men about their living and working conditions.

The Duke and Duchess of York driving through the streets after their wedding at Westminster Abbey in April 1923.

The news-reels didn't bother them very much and the press left them pretty much alone. There were two reasons for that which might seem on the surface to be contradictory:

1. The popularity of King George V, which had been slow in developing, was beginning that rise which was not to be stopped until at his death a whole Empire would stand silent in grief.

2. The popularity of the Prince of Wales was also beginning that rise which was not to end until the abdication came with the suddenness and unexpectedness of a cliff hurled into the sea by an earthquake.

There was no room in the public imagination for a third figure in the Royal setting, or at least not for a man. Queen Mary, of course, shared the nation's affection with her Royal husband.

The Duke and Duchess were content. They wanted to found a home with their own circle of friends and to give their energies to such services of State as fell automatically to the second son of the King.

But almost at once their domestic plans were interrupted by a trip to East Africa. During the latter part of 1924 and into the beginning of 1925 they toured that colonial melting-pot where the heritages of the war still linger like the heat of summer after the sun has gone down.

It was the Duke's first important visit as the representative of the King, and although he went at it with his usual energy he found that he was still diffident and that on official occasions his stuttering embarrassed him.

His wife helped him as much as possible. Only the keenest and most sympathetic observer would have noticed how she would take on the conversation when she saw his nerves tightening. Sometimes she would interrupt him and appear almost to contradict him so as to make him forget his agony. He had not yet won the battle which he had set out to do as a boy.

But his mind was taking in the problems of Empire just as it studied the problems of industry when he was at home. If on official occasions in Kenya he was stiff and diffident there was not a trace of this when he talked to minor officials and residents. He saw much, learned much and made many friends. When they returned home there was little excitement displayed by the British public. It was just another piece of work by a man who liked doing things well. The public had other things to think about.

Then came the fateful year 1926. Two things of enormous importance happened in the spring of that year.

In April a daughter was born to the Duke and Duchess of York and was named Elizabeth Alexandra Mary. She was born at No. 17 Bruton Street, Mayfair, the girlhood London home of the Duchess.

Elizabeth, Alexandra, Mary! Why did the happy parents choose those names? The answer is simple enough on the surface: Elizabeth in honor of the baby's mother; Mary in honor of her grandmother; and Alexandra in honor of her great grandmother 'the Princess from over the seas.'

I wonder if there was not more in the choice of 'Elizabeth' than that? The Prince of Wales had said over and over again that he would never marry. He was young and might change his mind but . . . supposing he held to his intention and supposing no son was born to the Duke and Duchess of York?

This little child, this curious little bundle of humanity in her mother's arms, would some day be Queen of England—not Queen by right of marriage to the King, but Queen in her own name.

Do you doubt that their minds went back to the golden age of Queen Elizabeth, when Shakespeare broke the frontiers of the mind and Drake turned the oceans of the world into English lakes? One need not even ask if these thoughts came to them. They were inevitable.

Yet the fond delight of the parents was to be shad-

Glamis Castle.

—Spencer Arnold.

owed almost at once. The thing which the Duke had feared had come to pass. He had talked to his father about it and to the men themselves. The long strike of the miners had culminated in a general strike.

It was hard for the young Duke to see the British workman, whom he knew as a friend and a patriot, stumbling into a crisis from which any disaster might emerge. Their baby was only a month old when the nation rocked with a struggle that was heavy with fate.

All the wisdom was not on one side, nor all the foolishness. The facile cry of 'the Reds' was raised by many Die-hards and there were not lacking national leaders who were for putting down the strike with an iron hand. And in the labor camp there were some who called openly for revolution and violence.

The Duke was furious with the cry of 'Reds.' Better than any member of the Royal family he knew the character of the British working men, with their tolerance, their common sense, their innate courtesy and their humor. Those nearest the Duke were startled at the transformation in him. His novitiate was over. He was meeting the onslaught of events and making up his own mind as a man.

In the end the British nation, with its usual good sense, decided the issue between the strikers and the Government. It was declared that no section of the community could hold up the business of the nation and that the Government simply would not have it. So peers and bank clerks and piano salesmen and vicars ran the trains and omnibuses and the strike collapsed. Neither the 'Shoot 'em down!' nor the 'Blow 'em up!' school was given a chance and the country resumed its normal routine.

I remember at that time running into my old friend who was then Commander Louis Greig. He had played a big part in molding the character of both the King's elder sons, being attached to them officially. He was profoundly impressed by the Duke of York's progress as a man.

'Mark my words,' he said, 'that young fellow is going to make himself felt. He is a slow starter like his father but by Jove, when they come into the straight he will be there when a lot of others have trailed off.'

I wondered since if Louis Greig had any premonition of coming events. I don't think so. It was simply the appraisal of character by a shrewd Scot.

As far as the Duke and Duchess of York were concerned the calm after the storm only lasted a few months. Before the year was out they were asked to go to Australia and New Zealand for an official tour which would take six months.

It meant leaving the baby behind. Six months out of the life of their little child! Six months out of their lives as parents! One does not need to pry into their hearts to know what they were feeling. I have no doubt that the Duke found time with a hearty curse or two to wish that the Empire wasn't so confoundedly far flung. As for the mother, every woman in the world knows what she was feeling.

However, orders were orders and off they went to the Antipodes. I must say they were very wise in one thing. They took along with them in attendance Field-Marshal the Earl of Cavan and his Countess.

Lord Cavan (for some mysterious and illogical reason called 'Fatty' in the war) and Lady Cavan are two of the finest and nicest people in England. An exploding bomb would not upset his good-humored imperturbability and she would find some virtue in the worst woman alive. They made a most congenial party and returned with the most affectionate feelings.

Again the Royal couple did their job well and looked the 'Aussie' and the New Zealander straight in the eye. If their hearts were at home a good deal of the time when they should have been telling each other how great the Empire was who can blame them? The friendships of that trip have endured to this day.

When they came home to Britain I went along as part of the London crowd to shout 'Banzai!' or what-

The King being crowned in Westminster Abbey. The Queen is seen seated on the left.
—Graphic Photo Union.

ever the Cockney equivalent of that may be. The Prince of Wales was at the station to greet them and rode in a separate carriage.

The London crowd cheered the Prince and was merely formally friendly to the Duke and Duchess. They had not won their position in the hearts of the British people nor did it seem that they ever would.

Shortly afterwards I went to an official luncheon in honor of the Duke. His reply to the toast in his honor was labored and painful. It was an embarrassment and an agony to us all. Looking at him then and listening to him one could only feel that he would never do more than play his part on the fringe of events.

We were forgetting two things:

1. The fierce determination of the Duke to conquer his disability of speech and to triumph over the ill-health that had ruined his naval career.

2. The woman whom he had married and whose confidence in him was as great as her love for him.

The years passed by.

In 1930 Princess Margaret Rose was born at Glamis Castle. Like her mother she was an August baby. There were murmurs of congratulation and sympathy from the public. After all it was nice for a little girl to have a baby sister but still it would have been better to have had a boy baby in line for the throne.

The worship of the man-child in Britain is intense even in the poorest circles. The birth of two daughters and no son is simply something that isn't done. None of which worried the Royal parents in the slightest. They had seen their vision—another Queen Elizabeth ruling over the British people—and they were glad the second child was a daughter who would not spoil that dream.

And so began a period of unadulterated happiness. If ever a family circle radiated happiness it was the one which the Duke referred to as 'myself and my three ladies.' They were a self-contained unit and produced their own amusements.

The Duke was good at making up plays. Little Margaret Rose developed into a terrifying mimic—particularly devastating to august personages. Princess Elizabeth was beginning to suspect that she was a young person of some importance and rather frowned on her sister's instinct to burlesque, while secretly enjoying it.

The Duchess kept the balance as mothers have always done. Once when the family went to Scotland an old retainer took off his cap, and addressing Princess Elizabeth, asked how the 'little lady' was.

'I am not a little lady,' said Elizabeth, 'I am a Royal Princess.'

'That is quite true, darling,' said the Duchess. 'You are a Royal princess but we still hope that you will become a little lady.'

The Scottish mother was not going to have any nonsense.

Previous to their Australian journey the Duke and Duchess had lived in White Lodge in Richmond Park. It was a beautiful place and the park delighted both of them. Unfortunately, though, it was not convenient enough for official purposes and after necessary negotiations they acquired 145 Piccadilly and moved into it after their return from Australia. It is the last house fringing on Hyde Park and they were to experience there the happiest days of their lives.

When the Prince of Wales, in his tragic broadcast farewell, stated that he had been denied one priceless blessing that his brother had enjoyed, he was referring to the home life which he had seen at No. 145. Not only were the Duke and Duchess and their children devoted to each other, but they found the greatest joy in their life as a family. They had many friends who came to their house and there was not one who did not come under the spell of the good humor and the high spirits and the basic kindliness of it all. After all life was being pretty good to them. They were kept busy with official duties, but when these duties were

A scene during the Coronation Ceremony in Westminster Abbey, May 1937.

—Graphic Photo Union.

finished they could withdraw to the privacy of their own home without the fierce, relentless limelight of public curiosity pursuing them. Do you wonder that their fondest wish would have been expressed in the words: 'May the gods allow this to go on to the end of our story.'

In the spring of 1935 they had the joy of taking part in the Jubilee of King George V and Queen Mary. Those of us who were in London at that time are not likely to forget that May morning when the beloved King and his Queen drove through the streets to the acclaim of endless thousands of people. It seemed as if the great heart of London could not do enough to express its affection for this man and woman who had come to mean so much to them.

The close affinity between King George V and the Duke of York added to the pleasure of both of them in the Jubilee. Basically they were very much alike. Their minds and natures were closely in tune. That Christmas King George V broadcast to the entire Empire. With that deep voice which seemed so personal he spoke to the people of the Empire as his family. A few weeks later the people of the Empire listened to the radio as the announcer spoke the words:

'The King's life is moving peacefully towards its close.'

The sunlight of May had merged into the deep darkness of a winter's night.

The King and Queen in the Royal Coach during the Coronation Procession.

—Central Press Photos.

Chapter Six

THE KING IS DEAD. LONG LIVE THE KING!

The Prince of Wales was no more. Edward VIII had become ruler of the greatest empire of all time.

There had been some fears that he would refuse the Crown. His untamed spirit might reject the heart-breaking discipline of the throne.

But Edward did not thwart his destiny. He may have echoed within his heart the cry of the late Pope who, when elected by the Cardinals, fell on his knees and asked for their pity as well as their blessing; but he did not show it.

Those of us who took any part in public affairs knew of the complications of his friendship with Mrs. Simpson, but the public was unaware of her existence and rejoiced unstintingly at their idol's rise to the supreme position.

As for the Duke and Duchess of York it meant, of course, less liberty; for since there was no Prince of Wales to take his share of official duties the nearest brother had to shoulder a great deal of the burden.

And then, at the end of 1936, came the anxious day leading up to the abdication.

The British people, kept in complete ignorance by their press of what was known throughout the world, woke up one day to discover themselves in the gravest constitutional crisis since Parliament challenged the authority of Charles I.

I do not choose to try and revive the emotion or the passions of those days. No-one has attempted to tell the full story of those eventful days without partisanship. No-one could have taken a detached view of it all at that time—or could do so even now. It will be years before the historian, insulated by time, will be able to piece together the whole story and apportion blame or credit in just measure.

Needless to say, the whole business had occupied the mind of the Duke of York long before its climax. He had held long and anxious conversations with his mother but they had felt that if things came to a head the King would accept the inevitable and remain on the throne.

Even when the crisis was openly before the nation and Mr. Baldwin was struggling for a solution with the young King, the Duke and Duchess of York were certain that things would come right.

'David will not give up the throne,' they said to each other again and again. 'He cannot give it up.'

Then the tempo of events took a swifter pace. Passions were rising. The tragedy of King Edward's position was exposed in all its pitifulness. The most loved young man in the world, who had won the hearts of continents, had not one real friend who could guide and influence him at that hour.

The Duke of York talked to him but devotion is not necessarily intimacy. They respected each other for the very difference in their qualities but they had never been in complete sympathy. Somewhere in Edward VIII the restless spirit of Edward VII had been born again. Somewhere in the Duke of York the quiet purposefulness of his father George V lived on.

The irresponsible sections of the foreign press, which had done so much to vulgarize and render inevitable the crash of the short reign, were filling their pages with scandal and intimate descriptions of the King who, they said, was so befuddled with brandy that he did not know what he was doing.

It was cruelly untrue. Tragic as was his decision, Edward VIII determined his fate with clear eyes. He knew that his action must shake the very foundations of the throne but he did everything possible to limit that damage and destroy none of the precious heritages of the throne.

I have been told that somewhere in those conversations Edward turned to his brother and said: 'Bertie, you will make a far better king than I could be.'

It was a genuine and almost heart-broken tribute from the King, who in some strange way had always seemed the younger of the two.

The Royal Family on the balcony at Buckingham Palace after the Coronation.

—Central Press Photos.

As I have written, the activities of 145 came to a standstill. The Royal family, like the whole nation, was caught in the paralysis of an incredible drama.

At home the Duke and Duchess talked in hushed tones.

They had accepted the dream of their daughter as the future Queen of England, knowing that she would be trained for the task and that in the intervening years she would be accepted by the people as their ultimate sovereign and thus surrounded with that glamor and interest which is inseparable from high place.

But now—something unbelievable had happened. With no preparation, with no warning, with no real love from the people, they might be asked to take the throne!

The nation would be divided and resentful. They might be regarded as interlopers. More than indifference, they might have to face coldness and even hostility.

And it would be the end of their freedom. That is what hurt. This happy house would be closed. The gates of Buckingham Palace would clang behind them. Never again could they live their own lives. They would try to keep their friends but would something divide them?

So the young couple talked into the early hours of the morning, feeling the horizon closing in on them, a little thrilled, more than a little unhappy, and strangely lonely.

Who doubts that in their hearts they also prayed as Abraham Lincoln did when the Presidency of the United States came to him?

Mr. Baldwin came to the House of Commons and told us of the irrevocable decision of the King to abdicate. That night Edward spoke to the world on the radio and with a brave voice cried 'God save the King!' In the early hours of the morning he stood on the deck of the destroyer, looking at the shadowed outline of the country which he had ruled for so short a time.

For the third time in a little over two years we swore allegiance in Parliament to the King, his heirs and successors.

It was announced that Albert, Duke of York, had decided to take the name of George VI. The heralds proclaimed it to the drizzling winter air. The newspapers all said that we could look forward to a good monarchy like that of George V. I remember writing in the *Sunday Graphic* a character sketch of the new King. The words almost refused to come. As a people we had been so deeply hurt that our voices were dumb and hearts weary.

That night a friend said to me at dinner: 'A week ago, if a messenger had come to you or me that the King wanted to see us, it would almost have seemed like a command from a god. Now. . . .' And he shrugged his shoulders.

One of the shrewdest observers of public affairs in Britain said to me the next day that the throne would never survive. 'The abdication was its death-blow,' he said. 'England will be a republic within five years.'

It was in that atmosphere that King George VI and Queen Elizabeth ascended the throne.

His Majesty King George VI at his desk in Bucking-
ham Palace.

Chapter Seven

IT WAS A RAW MARCH MORNING AND AS USUAL countless thousands had gathered from the four corners of the United Kingdom to see the maddest of all steeplechase races—the Grand National. In another couple of hours fifty men and horses would start on the incredible four and a half mile stampede across canals, ditches, and jumps that rise like cliffs to daunt all but the strongest jockey and the bravest horse.

I had walked half a mile or so to take a look at the first couple of hurdles. There was no-one about except an ordinary-looking workman in an old trench-coat and a cloth cap. He looked as if he had walked from Liverpool to have a day out.

Suddenly from far away there came the sound of cheering. The workman turned around and looked towards the stands. With a swift, unconscious dignity he swept his cap from his head and stood rigidly at attention. He did not see me and was unconscious of everything about him.

Unconscious of all but one thing.

The King had entered his box. That was the meaning of the cheering we had heard. It was too far to make out the figure of either the King or Queen but the cheering told the news.

The years fell away from the man. His shoulders had straightened, his heels were together and one saw as clearly as if it were back in the days of the war just one more Englishman who had fought in it.

The cheering subsided. The workman replaced his cap, took the sports paper from his pocket, sucked his pipe and started looking over the form of the horses. There was nothing to distinguish him from any of the 30,000 other cloth-capped fellows near the course.

I made my way back towards the stands. From a few feet away I saw King George VI for the first time. As Prince Albert and the Duke of York I had seen him a hundred times through the years—but now we were looking at King George VI.

No man could mount the throne of England and remain exactly the same person as before. But I was utterly unprepared for the change in him. All diffidence had gone. Those hesitant gestures which had been characteristic of his personality had been replaced by a sureness of movement and an ease of manner that would have marked him out if he had been surrounded by a hundred men.

He looked amazingly fit and as if he could have made a good job of it if a mount were offered him for the great race so soon to be run. A manner of authority is a subtle thing. Falsely assumed it can be ridiculous. Unaccompanied by considerateness it can be repellent. The young King spoke and moved like one born to high estate, conscious of his destiny yet gentle and courteous.

Where was his shyness which used to come between him and the world? Hundreds of people crowded to the very edge of his box and stared at him with eyes that missed nothing. He was apparently unaware of them except for that vivacity which is so often the mark of an inner excitement.

And gradually the truth dawned upon us all.

This young man had fought his secret battle. He had been called to the throne when it was deep in shadows. He had not asked for it, nor had he been prepared for it, and the silence of the nation had made the pealing bells almost a mockery.

Somewhere in those hours that he had faced the future he must have said: 'I accept the crown which my brother has laid down. I have come to it, not by the succession of the eldest son or the hand of death, but from the necessities of the people. I shall never look back. I shall never admit regret. I am the King and I shall be a king.'

Late that afternoon I struggled through the human mass that was crowding the cobbled pavements of Aintree and caught a train to London. All around me were excited voices living again the disasters and glories of that incredible race, which starts like a cav-

The King during a visit to the Hawker Aircraft Works in December 1937.

—Photographic News Agencies.

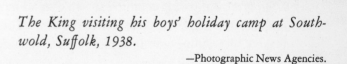

The King visiting his boys' holiday camp at Southwold, Suffolk, 1938.

—Photographic News Agencies.

alry charge and ends with three or four survivors battling it out for that last few feet when nothing is left but the bursting hearts of man and beast and the wild, joyous agony of the struggle for victory.

But my thoughts were on two men—the one who had become a king overnight and the one who had stood bareheaded in the distance to pay homage to his sovereign.

The King!

What is he but a man? Or is he perhaps less than a man since he has earned his place by birth and not by his own achievements? Is it not true that monarchies are a thing of the past and that kings and queens are but automatons like characters in a pantomime?

America is a republic, and Americans are known to be a very wise people who always have the best and most modern inventions. France, the home of reason, has long since abandoned the system of tyrannical, weak or dissolute kings.

The logic against monarchy is so overpowering. Who can seriously defend the choice of the eldest son even if you admit the principle of the Royal family? Logic, common sense, reason are all against it.

Then what is for it? The answer is—*human nature.* Nothing has been found to take the place of the monarchy. The reason it has fallen in so many countries is not the fault of the kings but of the people who were unable to blend the throne into a workable constitution.

And as I mused on these things in the jolting train I realized that of all the people in the world no-one understands the British monarchy so little as the wise, generous and intensely human citizens of the United States of America.

What is the King of England? Can you dismiss him as a mere figure-head who must meekly sign the edicts and laws which Parliament determines upon? What is his real position in the realm?

King George VI and Queen Elizabeth are the first lady and gentleman of the land. When the head of a foreign state comes to Britain they are the hosts. The Royal family are the only citizens of Great Britain who are completely divorced from politics. Their position is above the bickerings, suspicions and maneuvers of party warfare.

As the first family in the land they are expected to lead honorable lives, to be true hearted and to epitomize the virtues of the race. Thus there is a common bond between the monarchy and the people—the bond of family.

In their capacity of the first lady and first gentleman they will give the encouragement of their presence to as many worthy functions as time permits. They will visit hospitals, launch ships, attend charity *premières* and inspect new factories. In every way possible they will try to make industrialists, workers, and philanthropists feel that the nation acknowledges their service to the State.

Then there is the lighter side when at Ascot, the Courts and the garden parties at Buckingham Palace they encourage the pageantry of social life and recognize that England still maintains the tradition of aristocracy.

They shall take no public part in any controversy which racks the nation and, in return, the people will not subject them to the criticism, abuse or ridicule which is the normal reward of all others in public life. Unlike the Pope of Rome, who withdraws from all contact with ordinary life, the King mingles with the people and has his wife and children like the humblest worker—but yet he is a man apart from all others. The oath he takes is not unlike that of the Pope inasmuch as he renounces everything for service and gives up for ever the freedom which is the dearest possession of a man. Officially his duties are many and important. Not only is George VI King of England; he is King of Canada, King of Australia, King of New Zealand, King of Newfoundland, King of Ireland. Each of the

The King commencing his tour of the Duchy of Cornwall for the first time as Sovereign.

The King shaking hands with the Preston North End Team at the Wembley Cup Final in 1938.

Dominions is self-governing, with a representative of the King as the official link with the mother country. The Prime Minister of each Dominion, or the President of Ireland, has direct access to the King.

The value of that is obvious. Let us assume for the sake of argument that in Canada there is a Government of the extreme Right and in England a Government of the extreme Left. Ideologically those two governments might be antagonistic, not necessarily in general policy so much as in the method of approach.

Should a dispute arise between them the King can be of invaluable assistance. He can bring ministers into consultation and because of his presence and the tradition of decorum their discussions will be moderate in tone. Even as in the case of King George VI, when the monarch might be as yet politically inexperienced, the fact that he is non-partisan and a supporter of no faction brings reasonableness and dignity to the consultations.

Governments are impermanent things. They have their little day and then a wind rises from the sea and they are no more.

But the throne is permanent. It is a fixed unchanging star. Liberals succeed Conservatives at Westminster, Socialism claims its turn, Lloyd George is followed by a Bonar Law, and Ramsay MacDonald and Stanley Baldwin play musical chairs. Genius, caprice or disaster may throw up any man to be Prime Minister.

But the King goes on until his story ends and he is succeeded by the King. The whole undying permanency of the race is centered in the throne. The King is the symbol of our immortality.

As time goes on the occupant of the throne, in constant touch with his ministers, gathers an unequalled knowledge of public affairs. All government telegrams from secretaries of state are sent to him each day. He knows every secret. As he grows older his influence on his ministers becomes stronger because of his knowledge of the past. He must not suggest legislation or order his ministers to take a certain course but he can counsel, restrain and stimulate.

The position of the King is doubly important when a new government is formed. You must remember in such a case that the ministers who are just taking over have been in opposition, with all the freedom from responsibility which is one of the few compensations for being out of office. Suddenly they find themselves as the heads of departments while the former cabinet, rich in practical experience, prepares to riddle them with criticism. All their promises while in opposition rise up like ghosts to haunt and dismay them. They feel like interlopers and are far from being as jaunty as they seem.

Then each minister is received by the King, from whose hands he receives his title of office. A kindly, encouraging word . . . a reminder to look out for a certain danger that helped to bring down his predecessor . . . a bit of sage advice from an onlooker who has seen the whole game.

The minister departs from the palace with a new dignity. He is 'His Majesty's Secretary of State.' The mystic benediction of Royalty has fallen upon him.

Each officer in the Army holds his commission from the King. Every night at dinner in the officers' mess the toast is drunk, 'the King.' He is the head of every regiment. If there is a war it is the King who declares it.

It is 'His Majesty's Navy' that holds the routes of the seven seas. It is 'His Majesty's Royal Air Force' that guards the skies. 'At the King's command' the armed might of Britain goes to war.

By the prerogative of the King the Navy and Army are actually his own possessions. Every ship, every dockyard, every airdrome is legally and literally the property of the King. It is in his power to order the disbanding of Army and Navy.

But surely—the logical mind will cry—is this not

The King visiting the Duchy of Cornwall Estates in London, March 1937.

—Sport and General.

preposterous? Supposing the King were a fool or a villain!

That is where the British Constitution comes in. Unlike that of the U. S. A., the British Constitution is completely intangible, undocumented and absolutely workable. In other words everything is devised to make it possible for a good king to do a lot of good and a bad king to do very little evil.

Were the King to order his Prime Minister to disband the Navy, the Premier, if he tried to comply with the Royal Command, would be impeached by Parliament for 'giving bad advice to the Sovereign.' By this system no minister could carry out the King's command without being impeached. Therefore the Navy would not be disbanded.

Yet the King could still play his last card and dissolve Parliament, demanding that the country should be allowed to choose a government amenable to the Royal wishes. This would bring about a constitutional crisis which indeed might end the monarchy for ever.

On the surface there are grave risks in the enormous powers of the Royal Prerogative. In practice they are nullified. As I said before, the Constitution allows the King to do good but not evil.

No-one nowadays, except the completely uninformed or stupid, regards the King's position as a sinecure. Everyone realizes that he has a task which makes demands upon the whole personality, brain, heart and soul, and that to accomplish it successfully marks him as no common man.

It is difficult for people who lead normal lives to realize the daily life of an English king. He must sign every bill which passes through Parliament because, until his signature is affixed, it cannot become law. He reads reports of his Governors General, who write direct to the Sovereign. He must be ready at any time when the heads of states visit London to receive them and to give them hospitality, and also be thoroughly conversant with the problems of the particular nation concerned. Consultations with ministers are frequent and as head of the Established Church he must understand not only the personalities who control the destiny of the Church but also the problems which confront them.

He must maintain contact with the principal officials of the Court, who, while they administer his affairs, must receive his assent to anything that is unusual or in any way affecting precedent. There are the internal problems of the management of the Royal palaces, Windsor, Sandringham, Buckingham Palace, St. James's Palace and Balmoral. It is necessary that the Sovereign should study the debates in Parliament and be keenly aware of all the personalities which are dominating both the House of Commons and the House of Lords. The telegrams between the British Government and the Dominions and Colonies as well as all foreign nations are read so that at any moment, if he calls his ministers into consultation, he will know the situation intimately. One could extend this list indefinitely. Should he neglect any of his daily work it would cause serious delay. Should he make use of the information which he receives in any idle conversation or to unauthorized people it might cause the gravest embarrassment.

Unlike any other man, the King can never say after he has finished his administrative work: 'Now I am free and can do as I like.' Every morning his appointments for the entire day are placed before him. At 11.15 he and the Queen must leave for Guy's Hospital, where a new wing is to be opened. At 12.25 he must leave the hospital to go to the Mansion House, where there is a special Lord Mayor's luncheon at which a national appeal will be made. At 2.20 he must leave for the Palace, where 20 minutes later he has an appointment with the Archbishop of Canterbury. Every audience follows at absolute and mathematical intervals. At 5 o'clock he receives a deputation of world educationalists. It is necessary for him to know

The King leaving the Duchy of Cornwall Offices.
—Central Press Photos.

The King and Queen at the opening of the London Fire Brigade's new headquarters, July 1937.
—Topical Press.

their work, their hopes and their purpose for convening in England. At 8 o'clock there is a dinner at which the Prime Minister, the Lord Chief Justice, a visiting Dominion Premier and the Lord Chancellor, with their wives, will be guests. At 9.15 he and the Queen leave for the *première* of a new film which is to popularize the Air Force and raise funds for the National Playing Fields Association. Because of the presence of Their Majesties, tickets will have sold for as much as ten guineas each. Now the film *première* is over. What is left of the night belongs to the King and Queen. That is unless, as is often the case, they still have to read their correspondence.

The next morning the routine begins again. The life of an English King is one of complete devotion to duty and personal sacrifice. He has nothing to gain by being conscientious except the respect of his subjects. He cannot improve his position in the world. There is no glittering prize which can come to him, no increase of wealth, no new title. He gives up his life to the glorious but relentless demands of the nation. Even when it is possible for him to get away for a few days to Sandringham or Windsor with his family he cannot relinquish altogether the responsibilities of his position. The local church will expect him to attend and he will not disappoint them. Nor can he avoid the dispatch boxes which follow him wherever he goes. There is no village, no island, no country that he can visit and be alone.

It is a majestic thing to sit upon the throne of England. It is a glorious thing to represent the hope and pride of a mighty people, but the man who puts that crown upon his head knows its cruel weight. He must forswear liberty of action, freedom of expression and personal ambition. He is the center of a mighty and complex machinery of state. Should he falter or be untrue to the trust that is put in him the injury that he could do would endure long after he had ceased to exist.

The farmer on the Canadian prairies, the rancher in Australia, the settler on the South African veldt, the men who have gone across the seven seas and may never see Britain again. . . .

To them the throne is the star to which each one looks and finds his common bond of imperial citizenship.

When that workman took off his hat at Aintree and stood at attention he was paying homage to the young King in whose person all the pride and dignity and immortality of the race are centered.

More than a man in position and less than a man in human liberty, monarch and servant in one, trustee of the rich heritage of the past and guarantor of the immeasurable future, above the law, yet the assurance that justice will be done, the ruler of the people, the slave of the people and the embodiment of the people's immortality.

'Gentlemen—I give you the King!'

The Queen and Princess Elizabeth arriving at the Holborn Empire.
—Sport and General Press.

Her Majesty the Queen visiting the Mothercraft Training Centre at Cromwell House, London, June 1938.
—Sport and General.

Chapter Eight

ON WEDNESDAY, MAY 12TH, 1937, KING GEORGE VI was crowned in Westminster Abbey.

Those of us who were present are not likely to forget the splendor of the Coronation. London, Britain and the whole Empire were ablaze with excitement and joy.

What had happened to bring about this psychological transformation from the time the King ascended the throne to the time when the crown was placed upon his head? I have already described the silence and the weariness of spirit in Britain when the younger brother took over from King Edward VIII. Not only was there lack of enthusiasm, not only was there a feeling that something vital had passed from the life of the nation, but the young King was to experience a taste of the same heartless foreign press campaign which had done so much to bring down his predecessor.

There has sprung up a type of tabloid publication in America which is not important in itself nor in keeping with the dignity of the American press in general but which does not hesitate to disseminate unfounded rumors in order to increase circulation. Thus, having fed upon the unhappy private life of Edward VIII, it had to turn and see what it could find to expose in the life of King George VI and his family. Obviously the ordinary standards of sensationalism could not be satisfied. There was no secret romance to fill the columns. Therefore they turned to other things. It was said that the new King suffered from epilepsy. One publication, not content with that, stated that Princess Margaret Rose was deaf and dumb. These lies reached Britain, where credulity is not unknown. Much worry and much unhappiness were caused, and how could the King reply?

Once and for all, this is the truth about his health: As a boy he suffered from a duodenal ulcer and from appendicitis. The surgeon's knife cured him of both these things although it took toll of his health at the time. As he grew to manhood his health became steadily better. Like all the sons of King George V, he is athletic. His powers of endurance are extraordinary. He is today one of the fittest men in the world. The only illnesses he ever had were measles as a child and the trouble I have mentioned. There is not a single one of his subjects whose health is more established than his.

It seems almost cruel even to mention the attempt of his slanderers to reach his family. I know that the Americans, who are the kindliest people in the world, resented it as much as we did. It is sufficient to say that both Princess Elizabeth and Princess Margaret Rose are as charming and as healthy and happy and normal a pair of little girls as there are in the world.

While this slander went on there was quite rightly no attempt to offset it by giving a false glamor to either the King or Queen. The newspapers of Britain simply depicted them as the young man and young woman whom I have tried to describe in this book. Yet as the Coronation approached there was, on the part of the people, a surging of affection and enthusiasm towards them that has seldom been equalled in the story of the British race.

What was the meaning of it? What was the cause of it?

The British people are strangely psychic. They are more closely knit together than possibly any other race. They think as one man and feel with one heart more easily than any other people. Suddenly it had come to them that King George and Queen Elizabeth had taken on their high task because the country and the Empire needed them. While every coronation is a glorious festival, here was something entirely new. King George VI had come to the throne at a moment when the nation had been deeply and profoundly hurt; the throne had been gravely injured. And now we saw the truth that whereas other kings had mounted the throne by the right of succession, this young man, George VI,

*The Princesses Elizabeth and Margaret Rose, a recent
photograph.*

—Marcus Adams.

did so as the people's King, created out of the needs, the hopes and the prayers of the British race.

It is very difficult for citizens of other countries not to belittle, much less fully to understand, what the King and Queen mean to the lives of ordinary individuals in the British Empire. To the aristocrat they of course represent tradition, authority, stability; but to the common man, doing his best in a daily round which destiny has made 'crib'd, cabin'd and confin'd,' they mean romance and beauty, with which in some strange way he is identified. Their activities, their very existence, make his horizon larger—somehow make personal the strange intricacies of domestic and foreign affairs. In moments of stress the King's behavior is the keynote for the nation. When the ordinary man is called upon to leave home, mother, wife, sweetheart and children to endure hardship and filth and death in battle, it is the King whom he follows, because he represents what the nation stands for that gives it the right to demand such sacrifice. Under all the pomp and ceremony and glory that daily surround the King and Queen, and in which the people delight, under the spectacle of glamorous, carefree living that they present to the public gaze—perfectly dressed, perfectly groomed, smiling and gay—the people are bound to them by the knowledge that they too are inexorably tied by the responsibilities of their high calling, and confidently expect them, when need arises, to sacrifice personal inclinations. Like the humblest citizen they have given hostages to fortune, and are called upon, within the stern limitations laid upon them, to make life beautiful.

One definition of true art is 'the achievement of beauty within prescribed limitations,' and true kingship is just that. Scoffers may say that the monarchy is only a symbol, but the world today is closer to realizing the power and importance of symbols than it was at the turn of the century. Without symbolism life becomes drab and commonplace. Even the stark realism of communist and totalitarian governments has found symbolism essential to the accomplishment of their purposes.

The British, too, are essentially Puritans. Even if golf courses are crowded on a Sunday and motor-cars cover the country like a rash, the British are nevertheless religious. Therefore they saw once more at the head of the State the restoration of family life, the trinity of husband, wife and children. Besides that they sensed the personal sacrifice which King George and Queen Elizabeth had made to carry out the heavy duties imposed upon them by tradition and necessity.

One more thing stood out with stark clarity. To the people of Great Britain there is something which counts above all others—*character*. They have demanded it in public life and they have put it above everything else. In politics the most brilliant and fascinating personality has no chance unless he possesses the basic quality of character. It runs right through the life of the nation. The British found that in their young King and Queen they had two people richly endowed with purpose, with steadfastness and with responsibility.

Thus on that May morning when the King and Queen drove to Westminster Abbey the hearts of the populace went out to them as if to atone for the coldness of their attitude a few months back. The great ones of the earth gathered from all lands to do homage. The Dominions sent their ministers, the Colonies their representatives, the Arabs their chieftains, Japan its Crown Prince, America its Ambassador and so *ad infinitum*. Yet the tribute that meant most that day came from the people outside on the streets and from the outer Empire listening on the radio to the gorgeous music and the mysticism of the ceremony inside the Abbey.

There is no need now to describe in detail that marvelous day. The climax came when the old Archbishop of Canterbury faced the gallery where the Peers and

The King and Queen with Queen Mary and the Duke and Duchess of Kent after the Cenotaph Ceremony, Armistice Day 1938.

—Sport and General.

The King at Balmoral Castle.

—Spencer Arnold.

part of the Commons were sitting.

'Sirs,' said the Archbishop, 'I here present to you King George your undoubted King; wherefore all you who are come this day to do your Homage and service, are you willing to do the same?'

There came a mighty shout in response: 'God save King George!'

Three times more the Archbishop turned and asked the same question until from East, West, North and South there came that grand response: 'God save King George!'

Can literature or any of the imaginative arts create a scene more tense, more wonderful? And could Shakespeare himself have found words with a more resolute finality than 'your undoubted King?'

I cannot guess the thoughts of King George VI, but he must have been uplifted to the heights by that loyal cry four times repeated.

And thus it came that he was crowned in Westminster Abbey and wore upon his head the symbol of power and service which is heavy in substance and in implication.

As he watched, his two brothers knelt before him, touched his crown with their hands and kissed him on the cheek.

Pomp and pageantry if you like, but nothing without meaning.

Then did Her Majesty wear her crown, sparkling in the morning light, but not less heavy in its meaning than the one worn by her Royal husband.

It was all over. The King and Queen stood ready to depart, but the last great thrill was at hand. The trumpets sounded their call once, twice, a third time.

Then gently, very quietly, the choir began to sing 'God save our gracious King, long live our noble King.'

Peers and commoners, heads of foreign states and princes from the desert, stood at attention.

Do you wonder that there were many of us who could only remain silent, gripped by an emotion too deep for utterance?

The organ and the orchestra took up the anthem. Now it was no longer quiet. It was triumphant with hope, with belief in the future, with confidence and trust in the man who had been crowned King of the peoples of the British Empire.

There was a last long roll of the drum. The Coronation of King George VI belonged to history.

As this story of two young people nears its end I want to take you just a little further to a dull November morning in 1937. It was the day of the annual opening of Parliament and the King was to perform the function for the first time.

No news-reel or newspaper camera has ever been allowed to record the spectacle. Yet the theater could never offer anything so spectacular or dramatic.

Parliament is opened in the House of Lords because the King, not being a commoner, cannot enter the House of Commons. That business was settled when Charles I overplayed his hand against Parliament.

On this particular November morning we were gathered in the House of Commons, dressed in the dull clothes of our trade, when Black Rod, in black silk costume, arrived with an escort from the House of Lords—at which the door of the Commons was closed in his face.

Not to be outwitted, the visitor hammered with his mace three times upon the door.

'Strangers!' we duly shouted.

At this our own Black Rod, complete in knickers and black silk stockings and sword, went to the door. After the traditional parley it was announced that there was a messenger from the King and was it our wish that he should be allowed to enter?

'Aye!' we shouted, and the King's messenger, with deep bows to us (which we duly reciprocated), said that His Majesty would be opening Parliament in a

*The King and Queen at the unveiling of the Austra-
lian National Memorial at Villers-Bretonneux during
their visit to France in July 1938.*
 —Photographic News Agencies.

few minutes and would be glad to have his faithful Commons come along and see him do it. If the language was somewhat more traditional the meaning was just the same.

Accordingly a number of us formed a procession and marched down the famous corridor to the House of Lords, where we gathered at the Bar looking like the mob at the palace gates.

What a scene!

The *corps diplomatique* in their gold braided uniforms, the bishops in their gowns, the peers in their ermine cloaks and coronets and law lords in their gowns and wigs. In the one-row galleries on either side sat the peeresses in evening dress with tiaras catching and reflecting the light from the chandeliers.

The loveliness of the Englishwoman has no setting to equal that of the opening of Parliament when a blaze of lights defiantly turns morning into night. The feast of color stimulated the senses and sent the mind philandering with past ages when the ancestors of these women looked down where men jousted with death in the lists for the favor of a smile.

On the raised dais there were two empty chairs—for the King and Queen. Many of us recalled the lonely effect of the previous year, with one chair set in solitary and rather pitiful grandeur as Edward VIII opened the only Parliament of his reign.

Suddenly there was the sound of trumpets outside, and cheering. We knew Their Majesties had arrived.

Slowly the lights were lowered until the only illumination came from the windows where a grisly mist from the river was looking in like an uninvited guest. The pageantry was gone and we appeared like supers on the stage when the curtain goes down and the footlights are turned out.

Then there was another fanfare of trumpets. The lights blazed out once more and in the doorway stood the King and Queen.

As the House stood silently Their Majesties were led to their seats, where the King was handed the speech from the throne. This was a document of some 1200 words outlining the Government's legislative program for the coming session, a document prepared by the Government but read by the Sovereign.

Like most of the people there I suffered agonies waiting for the King to begin. For anyone to face that brilliant gathering would have been an ordeal, but with memories of his affliction when he had spoken as the Duke of York it seemed unbearably cruel.

The Queen glanced towards him with the suggestion of a smile and then looked straight ahead with a calmness which deceived no-one.

'My Lords and Members of the House of Commons.'

The King's voice was low and musical. A man's voice too, unusually rich and deep and strong. It filled the Chamber without the slightest effort.

'My relations with foreign powers continue to be friendly.'

The familiar words were spoken slowly but with no suggestion of hesitation or impediment. Every sentence was perfectly enunciated as the document proceeded.

Gaining in confidence, the King looked up to emphasize a point. I looked at his face, wondering what had changed it since the days not long back.

And then I realized it. This was the face of a man who had conquered. More than once he had cried out in anguish of spirit against the ill health which had robbed him of his career in the Navy, and the affliction of speech which had made his public appearances so harsh an experience.

There in the House of Lords he spoke as a man who had fought his secret battle and won, a man strong and lithe, a King who was the master of his fate.

No wonder in the Queen's eyes there was a look of pride which she could not have concealed if she tried. She had played her part in the secret battle and she was not ashamed to show her valiant pride in her hus-

The King being piped aboard H.M.S. Bittern, *1938.*
—Sport and General.

band. As for their subjects, from conservative to radical they have won regard and esteem. They have not made Britain 'lose face;' rather, they seem destined to gain wider laurels for her. It is a simple truth to say that Britons are proud of them—proud of the way they have assumed office and are adorning it with dignity, with ability and with charm.

'I pray that, under the blessings of Almighty God, the outcome of your deliberations may advance the happiness and well-being of my people and the peace of the world.'

It was over. The King and Queen left Westminster Palace and entered their golden coach to the cheers of the crowd. And I warrant that there were no happier young people in the world than these two whom destiny had so strangely called to the British throne.

The King and Queen driving to Thanksgiving service at St. Paul's.